1 9 9 5

COMMEMORATIVE

STAMP

COLLECTION

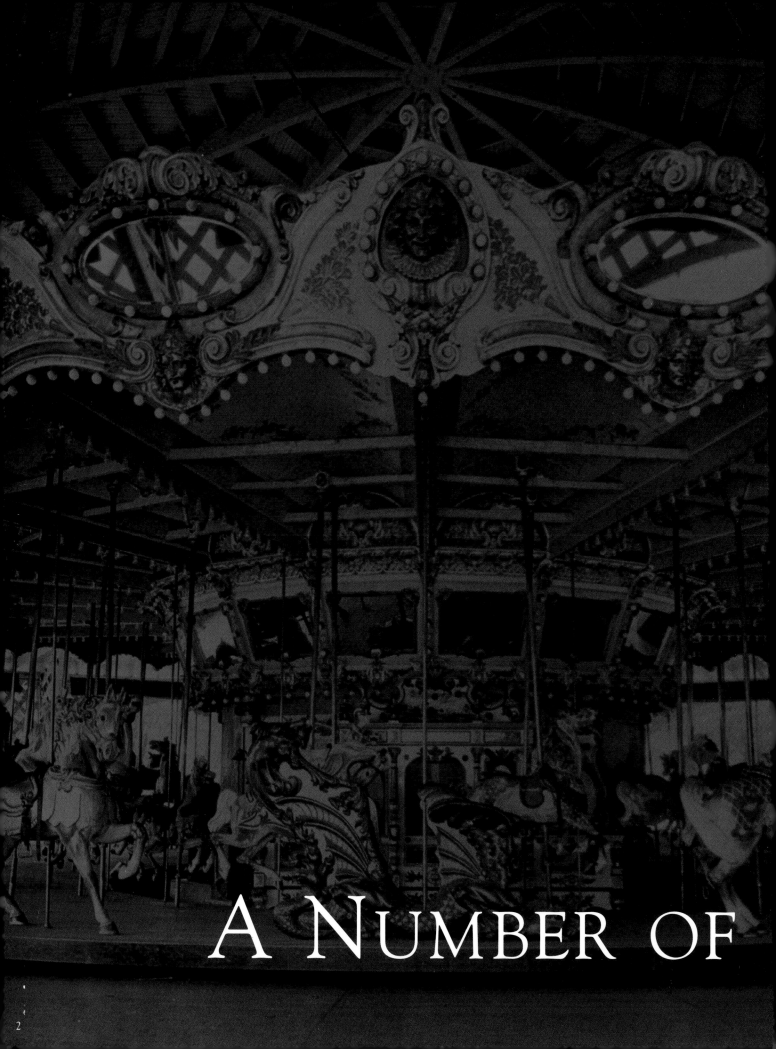

A Number of

What is it about the STAMP that draws so many to so small an object? They have become a licking, sticking, daily ritual for most; for others, a collector's miniature journey into the art, history and achievements of America. Yet, the results are quite the same — billions of colorful bits of glued paper criss-crossing our country every second...of every day...of every year. 1995 was an exceptional year. ● It began with a first-class rate increase from 29 cents to 32 cents — an increase that rendered the last 29 cent stamp and the year's first commemorative issue, the Lunar New Year, good for all of two days. Yet, despite the small rate increase, 27 new commemorative subjects totaling over 2,790,000,000 stamps were printed in 1995. That's a total of over 75 tons of those tiny little punched-out paper dots, known as "chad", that are produced in the stamp perforation process. ● Among the year's most notable commemoratives were the group of four honoring the 25th anniversary of Earth Day. Over 150,000 children, ages 8 through 13, entered the national stamp design contest which produced four outstanding designs (see page 12). ● Capturing the allure and charm of an American beauty like Marilyn Monroe, however, was no small task. Nine artists submitted over two dozen pieces of original art in an attempt to capture the

humor and beauty, glamour and sensuality that was Marilyn Monroe. The final selection resulted in 400,000,000 commemorative *Marilyns* that rolled off the presses and into the hands and hearts of millions. The star-studded stamp even included a star perforation in each corner instead of the standard round dot. Such a unique perforation pattern was a United States Postal Service first, and it resulted in a whopping 600,000,000 tiny perforated stars. ● For philatelists everywhere, the 27 new United States Postage Stamps issued in 1995 provide a wealth of new miniature works of art we lovingly know as commemoratives. Even amidst such advanced new high-tech methods of communication as E-Mail and the Internet, over 40,000,000,000 stamps flew from coast to coast over the course of the year. ● Credit goes mostly to the mail carriers, but also to the designers. This year, over 1,500 artist's portfolios were reviewed in the process of matching subject to designer. The final team of 28 talented designer/illustrators who brought these 27 issues to life can be found on pages four through seven. ● All in all, the year 1995 leaves stamp enthusiasts lots to look forward to. Whether you're a first time collector, or a seasoned philatelist, come...we have a little something to show you.

REASONS

TABLE OF CONTENTS

Clarence Lee
Honolulu, HI
Designer of all
three Lunar New
Year stamps
basing each on
Chinese paper cuts.

Laura Smith
Hollywood, CA
Received her
inspiration for this
issue from her
collection of early
poster stamps.

Melody Kiper,
Shreveport, LA;
Christy Millard,
Lakewood, CO
Jennifer Michalove,
Stonington, CT;
Brian Hailes,
Millville, UT;
(More than 150,000 kids
ages 8-13 entered this
design competition.)

Daniel Schwartz
New York, NY
A specialist in
portraiture, he was
recently awarded
the Altman Figure
Painting Prize from
the National
Academy of Design.

Chris Calle
Ridgefield, CT
Designer of more
than 25 U.S. and
20 foreign postage
stamps.

Terry McCaffrey
Leesburg, VA
Principal designer
for USPS philatelic
products for the
past 12 years and
Manager of the
Stamp Design
Group.

Recreational Sports	POW & MIA	Marilyn Monroe	Texas Statehood	Great Lakes Lighthouses	United Nations	Civil War
Jupiter, FL	Washington, DC	Universal City, CA	Austin, TX	Cheboygan, MI	San Francisco, CA	Gettysburg, PA
May 20, 1995	May 29, 1995	June 1, 1995	June 16, 1995	June 17, 1995	June 26, 1995	June 29, 1995

(21)　(23)　(25)　(26)　(28)　(30)　(33)

Don Weller
Park City, UT
A true competitor, Don is a winner of the Lifetime Achievement Award from the L.A. Society of Illustrators.

Carl Herrman
Ponte Vedra Beach, FL
Designer and former president of the American Institute of Graphic Arts, D.C. Chapter.

Michael Deas
New Orleans, LA
The pick of nine artists who submitted designs for this alluring subject.

Laura Smith
Hollywood, CA
A Mexican-American native of Sherman, Texas and designer of this second statehood issue of 1995.
(Designer's portrait with Florida Statehood stamp.)

Howard Koslow
Toms River, NJ
Designer of this, his fifteenth stamp, for the USPS.

Howard Paine
Delaplane, VA
Art Director of over 200 USPS stamps including "The King" (Elvis).

Mark Hess
Katonah, NY
Designer of this 20 stamp sheetlet, Mark's Legends of the West stamps were voted most popular in a national collector's poll.

TABLE OF CONTENTS

Paul Calle
Stamford, CT
The subject of two
books, Paul's works
are included in the
National Gallery
of Art.

April Greiman
Los Angeles, CA
A leading designer
noted for integrating
environmental,
motion and interac-
tive design formats.

Dean Mitchell
Overland Park, KS
A featured artist of
the PBS special
"The Living Canvas."

Bill Bond
Arlington, VA
A WWII veteran of
the British Royal
Navy, Bill designed
these, the fifth and
final series of
WWII's miniature
series.

Thomas Blackshear
Colorado Springs, CO
Co-designer and award-
winning illustrator who
really gets us in the
swing of things.
Dean Mitchell
Overland Park, KS
Co-designer
(See Louis Armstrong
stamp)

Ned Seidler
Hampton Bay, NY
A sequel to his 1994
summer flower
designs, Ned follows
up with fall.

Herb Kane
Captain Cook, HI
Designer, historian
and Pacific canoe
voyager.

Comic Strip Classics
Boca Raton, FL
October 1, 1995

Holiday Contemporary
North Pole, NY
September 30, 1995
Holiday Traditional
Washington, DC
October 19, 1995

U.S. Naval Academy
Annapolis, MD
October 10, 1995

Tennessee Williams
Clarksdale, MS
October 13, 1995

James K. Polk
Columbia, TN
November 2, 1995

Antique Automobiles
New York, NY
November 3, 1995

(48)   (51)   (52)   (54)   (56)   (59)

Carl Herrman
Ponte Vedra Beach, FL
Designer and one
of five USPS Art
Directors of stamps.
(Designer's portrait with
POW & MIA stamp.)

John Grossman
Laura Elders
Sausalito, CA
Designers,
Contemporary
Dick Sheaff
Boston, MA
Designer,
Traditional

Dean Ellis
Amagansett, NY
One of LIFE
magazine's "most
promising painters"
in 1950, Dean's art is
now part of over 16
public collections.

Michael Deas
New Orleans, LA
Designer and native
of Williams' noted
favorite, the
'Crescent City'
(New Orleans).
(Designer's portrait
with Marilyn Monroe
stamp.)

John Thompson
Waterloo, IA
A unique artist who
employs the "scratch-
board" technique
reminiscent of old,
turn-of-the century
engravings.

Ken Dallison
Mississauga,
Ontario, Canada
Known as the "auto
artist," Ken is also
the father of the
1988 Classic Cars
stamp booklet.

This year marks the Year of the Boar — the last of the twelve animals in the Chinese zodiac to mark Lunar New Year. A symbol of virility, the Chinese boar also has come to be a good luck token. In addition, the boar is purported to resemble the founding father of the Kitan — a people who migrated from Manchuria to rule large parts of North China about 1000 years ago. ● In celebration of Lunar New Year, the boar plays host to two weeks of Chinese festivities and rituals. The New Year festival is a gathering time for families whose sons and daughters travel from afar to mark the occasion. Before sitting down to a ritual feast, the father and eldest son visit the family graves to invite their ancestors to the home. Shortly afterward, pictures are hung in the home beside candles and incense while the doors are protected by the two genii of the door, as well as by other red symbols that guard against evil spirits. ●

In the streets, decorative lamps and lanterns, paper dragons and shadow-pictures invoke the hearth god. It is believed that the god ascends on the 24th day of the 12th month to report to the spirits all that it has witnessed over the past 12 months. Walls are adorned with brightly colored pictures that proudly display well-nourished, chubby children — a symbol of health. Finally, pictures of domestic spirits such as the god of riches and the goddess of mercy adorn the shops and windows around the cities and towns. ● The first full moon after the New Year marks the end of the two-week festival. This year's Lunar New Year began on January 31, 1995. This third issue in the ongoing Lunar New Year series honors the Year of the Boar and was the last of the 29-cent stamps to be issued before the rate increase that took effect January 1, 1995. ● This joyous Chinese paper cut design is offered with New Year's greetings from artist Clarence Lee of Honolulu, Hawaii, who has designed all three Lunar New Year stamps.

NEW YEAR

1995 一月 星期二

31

乙亥 正月 初一

喜神在正南方， 貴神在正東方， 炷香宜用子丑寅卯時

Background: Page
from Chinese Lunar
calendar

Inset, above: Boar
stamp

Opposite, top: Chinese
window hanging
wishes "Happy New
Year"

Opposite, left: Chinese
door-guard god com-
monly placed on doors
of houses to ward off
demon spirits during
the new year

Opposite, right: Street
dragon, Chinese New
Year celebration, San
Francisco

Our nation's 27th state was named by Spanish explorer Juan Ponce de Leon when he first saw this land during Pascua florida, the Feast of Flowers, at Easter 1513. Today, we know it as the United States' most popular vacation spot — with more miles of sunshine, beaches and coastline than any other state in the continental U.S. Each year, Florida is the favorite destination for millions of vacationers. Throughout this semitropical peninsula, tourists flock to such popular places as Disney World®; Cape Canaveral, site of the John F. Kennedy Space Center; Everglades National Park, home to thousands

of species of birds and wildlife; and Miami's famous Art Deco district. Yet the story of Florida's statehood is rich in both history and culture. • Florida was a Spanish colony from the 1500s through 1763. In 1565, St. Augustine, the nation's oldest continuously occupied European settlement, was established on the northeastern coast of the peninsula. In 1763, Spain traded Florida to the British in exchange for Cuba.

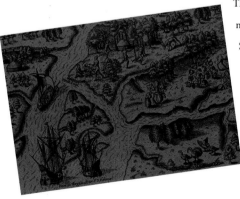

This trade, for what is now called the Sunshine State, was part of a larger peace treaty that ended the Seven Years War between Britain and France. The British then ruled the peninsula until Florida declared its statehood and entered the Union on March 3, 1845. Sixteen years later, Florida seceded from the Union to join the Confederacy in the nation's Civil War. Although much of Florida was won by Union forces early in the Civil War, the capital, Tallahassee, stayed under the control of the Confederacy until the end. In 1868, Florida was readmitted to the Union after a new constitution guaranteeing blacks the right to vote was established. •   In commemoration of the 150th anniversary of Florida's admission to the Union, this colorful "Gator," a long-standing icon of the state, was designed by Laura Smith as a tribute to the natural history and warmth of the Sunshine State.

FLORIDA

Place
Stamp
Here

Background: Fresh
Florida oranges

Inset, above:
Florida souvenir

Opposite, top: Florida
tourism poster

Opposite, center left:
Space shuttle
Discovery launch,
Cape Canaveral

Opposite, bottom left:
Explorer's map circa
1564

STATEHOOD

EARTH

Place
Stamps
Here

DAY

"The supreme reality of our time is...the vulnerability of our planet."

JOHN F. KENNEDY, 1963

Take a subject as important to children as protecting the environment; then invite over 40,000 schools nationwide to help spread the word. And what do you get? Over 150,000 ways to say "Save our Planet." ● In honor of the anniversary of Earth Day, thousands of eager students showed their concern for the future of our environment by pulling out their crayons, markers and colored pencils and submitting Earth Day stamp designs. Among the four winners, each serves as a reminder of the importance of such simple conservation methods as recycling, replanting, renewing and preservation. ● "An astonishing grassroots explosion," — that was how U.S. Senator Gaylord Nelson described the celebration of Earth Day just five years ago when over 200 million people on seven continents took part in efforts to promote land conservation, recycle renewable resources and improve disposal of hazardous waste. ● This year, in a collaborative effort to empower children to spread the word and commemorate this grassroots event, the United States Postal Service teamed up with McDonald's restaurants and over 40,000 schools to invite students to submit stamp designs. By participating in this nation-wide opportunity to express their creativity on behalf of the health and well-being of our planet, thousands of youngsters became ambassadors for a cleaner, safer Earth. ● Two winning entries from each state and the District of Columbia, formed the pool from which these four winning designs were chosen. The four winners were Melody Kiper (Litter), Brian Hailes (Tree Planting), Jennifer Michalove (Solar Power) and Christy Millard (Bathtub).

RICHARD

"The greatest honor history can bestow is the title of peacemaker...This is our summons to greatness."

RICHARD NIXON, INAUGURAL ADDRESS, 1969

Richard Nixon came to the presidency at a tumultuous time in our nation's history. Five hundred thousand American combat troops were fighting in Vietnam, the Cold War showed no sign of thawing, and the social fabric at home was coming apart at the seams. During his five and a half years in office, Nixon ended the war in Vietnam, negotiated the first nuclear arms limitation treaty with the Soviet Union, opened the door to the People's Republic of China, ended the military draft,

and restored peace to America's cities and college campuses. ● Nixon was elected to the House of Representatives in 1946. In 1950 he secured the largest margin of victory in the nation in winning election to the United States Senate from California. In 1952, he was selected the Republican nominee for Vice President and served for eight years under President Dwight D. Eisenhower. In 1968,

he was elected the nation's thirty-seventh President. ● President Nixon is most remembered for his foreign policy initiations, which planted the seeds for the end of the Cold War, the liberation of Eastern Europe, and the dissolution of the Soviet Union. His historic trip to Beijing in February 1972 ended more than twenty years of diplomatic isolation of the world's most populous nation. His strong military and diplomatic support for Israel during the 1973 Yom Kippur War helped

ensure Israel's survival. ● Nixon's domestic policy accomplishments, often overshadowed by his foreign policy successes, were nevertheless noteworthy. He established both the Environmental Protection Agency and the Drug Enforcement Administration, began the war on cancer, and brought about the peaceful desegregation of public schools in the south. ● Nixon was re-elected to a second term in 1972, carrying 49 states. His second term, however, was marked with an escalating battle to save his Presidency from the fallout from the Watergate break-in, an operation carried out by low-level operatives with the Committee to Re-elect the President. Eventually, citing the severe erosion of his political support in the Congress, President Nixon announced his resignation. On August 9, 1974, he left office, and was succeeded by Gerald R. Ford. ● In the years following his presidency, Richard Nixon wrote nine books and traveled abroad extensively. His many visits to the Soviet Union, China, Eastern Europe, and the NATO countries established him as a foreign policy elder statesman. His advice was actively sought by Presidents Reagan, Bush, and Clinton. ● On April 22, 1994, President Nixon died following a brief illness. He was buried with full military honors beside his wife, Pat, on the grounds of the Richard Nixon Library & Birthplace in Yorba

Linda, California. ● Traditionally, the Postal Service issues a memorial stamp in the year following the death of a former president. This stamp was illustrated by Daniel Schwartz of New York.

NIXON

Place
Stamp
Here

Background: Presid
and First Lady Pat

Insets: Nixon
campaign buttons

Opposite, left: Nix
in China, 1972

Opposite, right: Tir
"Man of the Year,"
1972

Opposite, bottom:
Nixon ponders

BESSIE

Place
Stamp
Here

COLEMAN

"...the Negro race is the only race without aviators and I want to interest the Negro in flying and thus help the best I'm equipped in to uplift the colored race."

BESSIE COLEMAN, 1925

She was intelligent, beautiful and eloquent. And before the flight in which she fell to her death on April 30, 1926, Bessie Coleman was a silent hero both of early aviation and of her own race. She had become the first African-American to earn the coveted international pilot's license issued by the Fédération Aéronautique Internationale in France. • Her dream, she said, was to be able to earn enough money to open her own flying school, "where aviators of any race could arouse their interest in the new, expanding technology of flight." But fulfilling that dream was not easy. • Coleman was born in a one-room, dirt-floored cabin in Atlanta, Texas, on January 26, 1892. When she was just two, her father, George Coleman, moved the family to Waxahachie, Texas, where he built the three-room house that became home to Bessie and her two younger

sisters. Soon after, her father moved north, leaving Bessie alone with her mother to tend to her two younger sisters. • But Bessie wouldn't settle for a life of daily chores or cotton picking. Assuring her church-going mother that she intended to "amount to something," Bessie moved to Chicago to seek a larger goal for herself. That goal became her pursuit of aviation. • Shunned by white pilots who refused to teach her to fly, Bessie found a willing sponsor in Robert Abbott, publisher of the nation's largest African-American weekly, *The Chicago Defender*. It was Abbott who suggested that she go to France, where, he claimed, she would not encounter such prevalent racism. Besides, he declared, "the French lead the world in aviation." • With the financial support of Abbott and others, Bessie left for France in late 1920. In just seven months, she completed her flight training and, on June 15, 1921, was awarded her F.A.I. (Fédération Aéronautique Internationale) license from France's best flying school. • The white press, accustomed to reserving attention of blacks to athletes and entertainers, finally took note of Bessie Coleman's achievement. It was the black press in the United States, however, whose weekly newspapers boasted of her airborne acrobatics and dubbed her "Queen Bess." • After fulfilling her lifelong dream of owning a JN-4 or "Jenny" (the World War I Army training plane), Bessie took off from Jacksonville's Paxon Field on April 30, 1926, to survey the area over which she was to fly and parachute the following day. With her seatbelt unfastened while she leaned over the edge of the cockpit to survey the area below, her plane flipped over and she fell a thousand feet to her death. • Bessie Coleman lives on as a hero of both black history and early aviation in this addition to the Black Heritage Series by Chris Calle of Ridgefield, Connecticut.

The Elite Circle and Girls DeLuxe Club
expect you and your friends to enjoy
'An Aerial Frolic'
honoring
Miss Bessie Coleman
Sat. May 1, 8:30 to 12 P. M.   Pythian Auditorium
Subscription 75c
Music by the Imperial Jazz Orchestra

NON-DENOMINATED:

FEBRUARY 1, 1995

VALENTINES,

VIRGINIA

DENOMINATED:

MAY 12, 1995

LAKEVILLE,

PENNSYLVANIA

Background:
"Amor and Psyche,"
Antonio Canova,
1787-93

Inset, above: "The
Kiss," Constantin
Brancusi, 1908

Opposite, top left:
"Les Amoreux aux
Marguerites," Marc
Chagall, 1949

Opposite, right:
"The Kiss," Gustav
Klimt, 1907

Opposite, bottom: "La
Cathédrale," Auguste
Rodin, 1909

Place
Stamp
Here

Place
Stamp
Here

Place
Stamp
Here

love possesses the power and passion, tenderness and touch that has so inspired generations of artists. ● From the painting of Raphael come these two charming angels. Replicated from his portrait of the Sistine Madonna, painted in 1513, these winged messengers are taken from beneath the Madonna and child, where they are pictured awaiting their task of ascending with Pope Julius II to the gates of heaven. ● No single stamp carries so popular a sentiment to so many people as Love

What is it about love that so inspires the heart? We fall in love, often forever. Love is eternal, yet it changes. ● For centuries, love has been a captivating, elusive feeling expressed through every kind of fine art — the paintings of Raphael, the windows of Chagall, the sculpture of Rodin and the arresting works of innumerable other artists. Within each work, as in life, love takes different forms of expression — a look in the eye, the touch of a hand, a first kiss, the union of marriage. ● Perhaps the universal message is that, despite war, hunger, strife, poverty and loss, there is always love; and where there is love, there is hope. Among all our emotions, none but

stamps each year. These charming winged messengers will accompany millions of letters, holiday cards, and invitations. As it has been throughout the ages, love is once again expressed here through a work of art — a powerful medium for the most heartfelt of messages. ● Designed by Terry McCaffrey of Leesburg, Virginia, the 32¢ messenger of love was issued in its non-denominated form in time for Valentine's Day from Valentines, Virginia. The two denominated versions were issued in time to adorn the June wedding season invitations.

RECREATIONAL

WHAAACK! THUMMMMP! CRACKKK! RRROLL! ACE! Remember the first time you swung that bat? Birdied a hole? Bowled a strike? Served an ace? Spiked one over the net? ● For competition or just for fun, participating in recreational sports has become part of the vital activity of our lives — celebrated by millions in such popular sports as golf, tennis, softball, bowling and volleyball. ● Golf formally made its way onto the mainstream American sports circuit shortly after the turn of the 20th century. Once reserved for elite members of the country club set, the game of golf quickly transcended class boundaries and exploded onto the national scene when All-Americans like Bobby Jones inspired scores of Americans to make this challenging game a part of their recreational lives. Today, over 25 million Americans participate in recreational golf for the challenge of this historic game. ● Tennis, the most international of sports, was, like golf, reserved for the very wealthy. In the 1920s, however, the immense popularity of such tennis stars as "Big Bill" Tilden and "Little Bill" Johnston inspired a rapid increase in public tennis facilities. Today, singles and doubles tennis play is recognized around the world as one of the most popular recreational sports.

● However, no recreational sport has been as prominent a part of our lives as the sister sport of baseball — softball. Played with a larger, softer ball and employing an underhand pitch, softball today is played by schools, churches, companies, local pubs and park districts in leagues and tournaments. ● If you think knocking one out of the park is tough, imagine knocking down ten pins twelve inches apart with a ball held using only three fingers. Today, that's what more than 50 million

Americans consider their kind of fun. Bowling, which in some form dates to the age of the Egyptian Pharaohs, was organized formally in the United States in 1875. In fact, even as far back as the 1860s, President Abraham Lincoln enjoyed taking a break from his duties to bowl a few frames. ● About 40 years later, William G. Morgan created a variation on the game of badminton — a sport called "Mintonette." After observing it in 1897, Dr. A.T. Halstead suggested it be named "Volleyball" and, sure enough, it was a winner. Fifty years later, America's servicemen and women popularized volleyball overseas during World War II. Then, in 1947, the International Volleyball Federation was founded. In the 1970s, beach volleyball became popular and the U.S. Outdoor Volleyball Association was formed. ● In commemoration of the 100th anniversary of the introduction of volleyball, the American Bowling Congress and the U.S. Golf Association's first championship, and in recognition of the millions of inspired amateur athletes who make these recreational sports a part of their lives, designer Don Weller of Park City, Utah, has captured these five moments in tribute to the physical enjoyment of recreational sports.

SPORTS

Place
Stamps
Here

POW

Among the saddest controversies related to America's participation in foreign wars is that surrounding prisoners of war (POWs) and individuals missing in action (MIAs). ● According to the Geneva Convention of 1949, prisoners of war are entitled to "special protections from mental and physical torture or coercion and are required to give their captors only their name, rank, service number, and date of birth." In addition, they are entitled to food and medical treatment as well as mail. Over the years, most countries claim to have complied with the rules regarding POWs, which are watched under the supervision of the International Red Cross. However, in every foreign war, servicemen have endured numerous violations. ● America's MIAs carry with them an even more troubling past. The United States Department of Defense, POW/MIA Office laboriously attempts to piece together information from photos, sightings, letters and battle accounts in an ongoing effort to identify these missing heroes. ● Though there are fewer POWs and MIAs from the Vietnam War than from either World War II or the Korean War, their fate has stirred enormous controversy. Twenty years after the end of the Vietnam War, opinion remains divided over whether Americans were held after the war ended. ● The United States Senate created a Select Committee on POW/MIA Affairs in 1991 to investigate POW/MIA questions. In 1993, the Committee reported that some POWs may not have been returned at the end of the Vietnam War, although there was no evidence to suggest they were knowingly left behind. Neither did they find any compelling evidence to suggest that American prisoners are still alive in Southeast Asia. ● Both federal and family organizations continue to work to discover whether these brave American servicemen and women are alive or dead and strive for the recovery and repatriation of American remains.

● In eternal tribute to the names that we remember on bracelets, on I.D. tags and in our hearts, Carl Herrman of Ponte Vedra Beach, Florida has designed this salute to our American POW/MIAs based on an original design concept by Gary Viskupic.

& MIA

Place
Stamp
Here

MARILYN

She was America's blonde beauty. Standing five feet, five and a half inches tall with dreamy, gray-blue eyes and a high-pitched voice, she spoke in a breathless whisper. She was funny, sexy and one of the most celebrated women of the silver screen. We knew her as Marilyn Monroe or simply Marilyn, an icon who lives on in the hearts of all those who have been touched by her films and her story. ● Marilyn was born Norma Jeane Mortenson on June 1, 1926. After dropping out of high school in the eleventh grade, Norma Jeane went to work assembling airplanes in Van Nuys, California, during World War II. It was there that an Army photographer selected her to pose for an article on women workers for *YANK* maga-

zine. ● It wasn't long before Johnny Hyde, a talent scout with the William Morris Agency, took notice of Norma Jeane and arranged her first silent screen test with Ben Lyon of Twentieth Century Fox. It was Lyon who suggested Norma Jeane change her name to "Marilyn"— a name he believed more befitting an actress. She chose her mother's maiden name, Monroe, and on August 26, 1946, Norma Jeane became Marilyn Monroe. ● Her goal, she said, was to get a motion picture contract — and that she did. Rising through small parts in two 1950 films, *The Asphalt Jungle* and *All About Eve,* Marilyn was cast in the role of the young, sexy woman matched with the more worldly man. By 1954, Marilyn's

popularity had increased significantly after her performance in *Gentlemen Prefer Blondes.* However, her storybook marriage to baseball star Joe DiMaggio ended in divorce that same year. Soon after, she ventured overseas on a tour of U.S. Army posts in South Korea, where her image as a sex symbol became international. That year, she appeared in perhaps her most stereotypical role as Fox's "Blonde Bombshell" in *The Seven Year Itch.* ● Marilyn quickly became discouraged by Hollywood's continued efforts to cast her merely as an object of desire. Determined to become a more serious actress, she moved from Hollywood to New York to study under the direction of Lee Strasberg. There, she worked to dispel her "dumb blonde" image and earn respect as a leading lady. ● In June of 1956, Marilyn married playwright Arthur Miller. It was during this period that she starred in some of her most popular films, *Bus Stop, Some Like It Hot* and *The Misfits.* ● Unable to rebound from the ills of her past or the stereotype that dogged her, she died from an overdose of sleeping pills at age 36. ● In tribute to this icon of the American screen, illustrator Michael Deas of New Orleans, Louisiana, brings back the wit and smile of Marilyn once again.

MONROE

™

Background:
Portrait of Marilyn

Opposite, top:
Spectators gawk in
Times Square as a
52-foot figure of
Marilyn is erected
on the front of
Loew's State Theatre,
May 1955

Opposite, left:
Marilyn's early
modeling comps,
circa 1946–48

Opposite, bottom:
Reaching for the
stars, promotional
photo from
*Gentlemen Prefer
Blondes,* 1953

Place
Stamp
Here

25

Place
Stamp
Here

Background: Herd of
cattle

Inset, below:
Legendary Texas
Ranger badge

Opposite, top: Ten-
gallon cowboy hat

Opposite, right:
Cattle drive

Opposite, center:
Texas bluebonnets,
Llano County

Opposite, bottom:
Don't forget your
spurs!

TEXAS

They call it the Lone Star State — the land where legends of the Old West were born. A land so vast and wide it stretches over seven hundred miles from east to west and nearly a thousand miles from north to south. Texas is the second largest state in the Union, a gateway to Central America and the home of two recent Presidents. ● They say it got its name from the Spanish and Indian words "tejas" and "techas," meaning "friends" or "companions." Yet, before Texas became a state, it was an independent republic — separated by war from Mexico on March 2, 1836. This new republic was soon struggling with Indian wars, raids by Mexican forces and financial problems. It was then that the cadre of legendary lawmen we know as the Texas Rangers appeared, to uphold law and order.

● In September, 1836, Texans finally opted for annexation by the United States, but approval by the U.S. Congress didn't come until 1845 because the northern states were opposed to slavery. The U.S. Congress finally accepted the Texas state constitution on December 29, 1845, and Texas became the nation's 28th state. ● To join the Confederacy, Texas withdrew from the Union on February 1, 1861. There was little fighting in Texas during the Civil War, although notable battles included the capture and recapture of the port city of Galveston. The final battle on Texas soil occurred at Palmito Ranch near Brownsville after General Robert E. Lee's surrender at Appomattox. ● After ratifying the 13th, 14th and 15th amendments to the U.S. Constitution, Texas was

readmitted to the Union on March 30, 1870. ● As cattle ranching became increasingly important to the economy, large herds of Texas Longhorns were soon driven over the Chisholm Trail through Oklahoma to the railroad in Kansas. ● In commemorative tribute to Texas statehood, designer Laura Smith, a Texas native, has captured the spirit of the Lone Star State with this gallant horseman carrying the Texas state flag.

STATEHOOD

Place
Stamps
Here

Background:
Seven-foot-wide
Fresnell lens from Split
Rock Lighthouse shines
for 22 miles

Overlay: Magnetic
navigation compass

Inset above: Detail of
St. Joseph Pierhead
Lighthouse

Opposite, top: Split
Rock Lighthouse
keeper Franklin Corell,
1930, beside giant
Fresnell lens

Opposite, left:
Schematic blueprint
of Spectacle Reef
Lighthouse

Opposite. right: Great
Lakes region map

GREAT LAKES

They stand alone — high above the sheer bluffs, along the sandy coasts and at the quiet ends of lengthy piers dotting the nation's Great Lakes. Yet, for the wayfaring mariner, they were swirling, flashing beacons of hope. They are the historic lighthouses of the Great Lakes — bound together by a mission to provide life-supporting light and safe passage, yet separated by vast waters whose inclement ways claimed the lives of many. Through dense fog, violent storms, winter gales and solid ice, these lighthouses stood as the guardians of the country's expanding commerce on the Great Lakes. ● These five lighthouses represent more than 220 that dot the bluffs, inlets and islands of the U.S. waters of the Great Lakes. The five are Split Rock Lighthouse on Lake Superior, St. Joseph Lighthouse on Lake Michigan, Spectacle Reef Lighthouse on Lake Huron, Marblehead Lighthouse on Lake Erie and Thirty Mile Point Lighthouse on Lake Ontario. ● In loving praise of the history, art and rich culture that surround these American icons, illustrator Howard Koslow has brought new life to the enduring legacy of these five U.S. Great Lakes lighthouses.

LIGHTHOUSES

UNITED

Place
Stamp
Here

Background: U.N.
General Assembly

Inset, below: U.N.
flag pin

Opposite, top left:
U.N. commemorative
button

Opposite, top right:
U.N. world headquar-
ters, New York City

Opposite, center left:
Kindergarten children
in Fayum, Egypt

Opposite, bottom:
Portrait of an elderly
woman, Koki,
Cambodia

NATIONS

"The heroes of the world community are not those who withdraw when difficulties ensue, not those who can envision neither the prospect of success nor the consequence of failure — but those who stand the heat of battle, the fight for world peace through the United Nations."

HUBERT H. HUMPHREY, 1965, NEW YORK CITY

It is a worldwide symbol of peace, relief and hope. A coalition of 185 nations bound together in the pursuit of peace, humanitarian effort and enlightened self-interest. It is the United Nations — now celebrating the anniversary of its fiftieth year. ● Founded at the close of World War II and established in the spirit of the

League of Nations, the United Nations has been actively engaged in numerous humanitarian and peacekeeping missions around the world. These began with the deployment of peacekeeping forces in the demilitarized zone between North Korea and South Korea in 1953. Since then, numerous food, medical and peacekeeping missions have been stationed in such countries as Haiti, Bosnia, Somalia, the Congo, Cyprus and in many regions of the Middle East. From food for starving children to medical aid for disease-ridden areas, the U.N. often has provided the only beacon of hope in

aiding millions of refugees around the world. ● Among the U.N.'s daily duties are the issues addressed by the General Assembly — an international forum for debate that exists to prevent worldwide conflict. Its efforts have led to the Convention on Genocide in 1948, the Outer Space Treaty of 1967, the Nuclear Nonproliferation Treaty of 1968 and the Seabed Treaty of 1971. It also serves to aid economic and technological advancements in developing nations. ● With the cold war over, the U.N.'s role has become increasingly important to preserve and restore peace in such war-torn areas as Kuwait, Cambodia and Somalia. Additionally, the U.N.'s many affiliated humanitarian groups, including the Food and Agriculture Organization, the World Health Organization and the Office of the United Nations' High Commissioner for Refugees, all play an essential role in maintaining world health and food assistance. ● The current United Nations Secretary-General is Boutros Boutros-Ghali of Egypt, the first African to serve as Secretary-General. ● This commemorative stamp, designed by Howard Paine of Delaplane, Virginia, honors the fiftieth anniversary of the founding of the U.N. and features the international seal of the United Nations, reflecting world peace and cooperation.

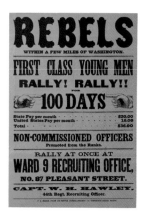

The most traumatic single event in the history of the United States was America's Civil War — a war seen by millions down the long barrel of a loaded rifle. ● No one on either side, North or South, could have predicted such horror. When the last shot was fired, a total of more than 3,525,000 men had engaged in more than 10,450 battles and skirmishes. With fighting from as far as Vermont to the north, Texas to the south, and the Arizona Territory to the west, the Civil War raged from 1861 to 1865. ● During those four long years the daily death toll averaged 451 soldiers — in battles like Gettysburg, Shiloh, Vicksburg, and Chancellorsville, to name a few. Lands were scorched, cities overrun, farms destroyed and once wide open fields and wooded forests of the nation's southeast were laid to waste by the war. ● Brothers drew swords against brothers; fathers and sons took opposite sides. From the Union side came legendary figures — President Abraham Lincoln, father of the Emancipation Proclamation; Generals Ulysses S. Grant, William Tecumseh Sherman and Winfield Scott Hancock; Vice Admiral David Farragut; Union nurse Clara Barton; abolitionist Harriet Tubman and orator Frederick Douglass. ● From the heart of the Confederacy came another drum roll of actors in history — President Jefferson Davis; Generals Robert E. Lee, "Stonewall" Jackson and Joseph E. Johnston; Brigadier General Stand Watie; Rear Admiral Raphael Semmes; diarist Mary Chesnut; nurse Phoebe Yates Pember. ● Out of the legendary lives they led emerged a new Union, with the promise of equality for the country's former Negro slaves. Yet, a high price was paid for that destiny of freedom for all. ● One of every five soldiers who served in the Civil War died in service – over 623,000 Americans – more than have perished in any other war in American history. Eventually, with great hardship, the Civil War's aftermath of hate began to fade. Veterans on both sides returned to the great battlefields to exchange stories, relive deeds of bravery and revere their fallen enemies. ● This release of 20 stamps by artist Mark Hess of Katonah, New York, joins the other U.S. Postal Service Classic Collections and honors the history of the nation's Civil War.

Background: A soldier's story by letter

Top left: Confederate recruiting poster

Right: Union forage cap and CVD picture frame

Bottom left: Union cavalry and artillery bugler jackets

Camp California
near Alexandria
Virginia Dec. 19. 1861
Dear Father Sisters and
Brother i received your
letter on the 19th and
is glad to hear from you and
u was verry long in answering
y last i am in good health a
sent there are a great man
the hospital now sick and
e has died i had the pleasure
seeing a baloon going of be
it started at Cloudes mill
bout half mile from us we
were alarmed on Wedensday n
last about 10 oclock and ordered
turn out for the enemy so we
up in line and then

Place
Stamps
Here

CAROUSEL

ackground: Carving
way, workshop of
.C. Illions

set, above: Carving
ols

pposite, top left:
ough mallet

pposite, top right:
dvertisement for
rmitage Herschell
o., makers of
eam-powered
rousels, 1899

pposite, bottom left:
raftsman polishes up
tual-size sketch for
upcoming horse

*pposite, bottom
ght:* Stein and
oldstein carved and
inted horse,
rca 1912

Place
Stamps
Here

HORSES

Remember the days when you scrambled aboard those great carousels in search of that one horse that you just had to ride? For all of us whose youth included visits to carnivals, trolley parks, circuses or state fairs, the carousel has been a lasting symbol of childhood amusement. ● In artistic tribute to the unique beauty of the American carousel come these four outstanding American Carousel Horses. The four horses chosen represent the three styles of American carousel carvings that were developed from 1870 to 1930 during the golden age of the carousel. ● Representing the flamboyant *Coney Island Style* is a magnificent "King Horse," adorned with tassels and a festoon of large cabbage roses. This elaborate horse was carved in Brooklyn, New York, by Stein and Goldstein, circa 1910. ● An excellent example of the realistic *Philadelphia Style* is the Indian Pony,

decorated with feathers, beads and tooled leather straps. The horse, circa 1905, was carved in Philadelphia by the great Daniel Muller, who is revered for his elegant, lifelike horses. ● Also included is a "Lillie Belle" jumper carved in the *Country Fair Style* around 1917. This stylized horse with a dramatic, high-flying mane was produced by the C.W. Parker Company of Leavenworth, Kansas, and was designed for portable carousels that traveled throughout the rural counties and towns of America. ● The final horse is an intricately designed armored jumper, circa 1912, also carved in the *Coney Island Style*. This medieval horse, draped with fish-scale armor and layers of chain mail, is another fine example of the carving skills of Stein and Goldstein. ● These prancing stamps were designed by Paul Calle of Stamford, Connecticut.

WOMEN'S

I WISH MA COULD VOTE

SUFFRAGE

Vote for Woman Suffrage Nov. 2, 1915

You ask us to walk with you,
Dance with you, marry you,
Why don't you ask us to Vote with you?

It all began one July morning back in 1848. A group of 300 women and men gathered in Seneca Falls, New York, to discuss women's rights. It was a Declaration of Sentiments and Resolutions that proclaimed, "It is the duty of the women of this country to secure to themselves their sacred right to the elective franchise." ● With this meeting, the women's rights movement was born — a movement that would see over 70 years of struggle to secure a woman's right to vote. ● Word of this new movement began to spread, and slowly, support for women's rights grew. Resistance among men, however, remained strong. Few men in those days acknowledged a woman's right to do much more than tend to her household duties. In fact, in 1868, men went so far as to add the word "male" to the Constitution's 14th Amendment, which defined the rights of a voting citizen. Even amidst the new freedoms won at the close of the Civil War, the 15th Amendment gave voting rights to emancipated men, but not to women. ● In fury and protest, the American Woman's Suffrage Movement was officially organized in 1869 and began its nationwide mission to mobilize women in support of their right to vote. Among their members came a new leader — Susan B. Anthony. After more than 15 years of dedicated struggle, the women's suffrage amendment was finally voted on in 1887. ● It lost. ● Male opponents called women's suffrage

"a menace to the home, men's employment, and to all business," and warned it "could double the irresponsible vote." Despite this setback, suffragists spent the next 30 years campaigning in both the states and territories. ● In 1916, Alice Paul, a leading suffragist who favored more drastic public outcry, founded the National Woman's Party. Along with her own band of loyal suffragists, they picketed the White House in 1917 with signs that read, "How long must women wait for liberty?" Following their arrest, they were sent to jail, where their ensuing hunger strikes caused a wave of public support to end their suffering and garnered new support for the movement. ● Two years later, on May 21, 1919, the House of Representatives finally passed the federal Woman Suffrage Amendment, and on August 26, 1920, the

amendment was signed into law after ratification by 36 states. The text of the amendment was exactly as Susan B. Anthony and Elizabeth Cady Stanton had originally authored it: "The right of citizens of the United States to vote shall not be denied or abridged by the United States or by any State on account of sex." They were just 28 words, but they formed the 19th Amendment to the United States Constitution which, at last, guaranteed women the right to vote. ● In honor of the passage of the 19th Amendment, designer April Greiman of Los Angeles, California, presents this historic commemorative stamp as a legacy to those who devoted their lives to winning this fundamental right.

LOUIS

They called him "Satchmo," "Dippermouth" and "Pops."

● Perhaps more than any other musical figure in jazz, Louis Armstrong left a legacy that equates the man with the music. It was his big, fat tone, his commanding presence and his bright smile that lit up stages from New Orleans to New York with a whole new sound.

● Born Louis Armstrong in a "Back o' Town" section of New Orleans on August 4, 1901, he went on to become America's most popular jazz cornet and trumpet soloist. ● At the age of 13, Louis Armstrong began playing in the brass band of the New Orleans Waifs' Home for Boys. After playing as a cornetist in both New Orleans and Mississippi riverboat bands, Louis broke onto the emerging jazz scene when he joined the King Oliver Band in Chicago in 1922. After impressing New York band leader Fletcher Henderson with his improvisational skills, Louis was invited to join Henderson's band in 1924. Frustrated by the short length of the solos afforded him, Armstrong returned to Chicago to start his own group, the "Hot Five" (occasionally "Hot Seven"). This group produced a number of prized recordings that today represent some of the finest examples of the classic Chicago Dixieland Jazz.

● In the early 30s, Armstrong made the first of many successful European tours. His unique brand of improvising and "scat" singing gave Louis multi-faceted appeal that landed him roles in films, on radio and later in television. This early style of jazz vocalizing involved imitating the sounds and phrases of the instrument. With his deep range and raspy vocal quality, Louis could switch from trumpet to voice in such classics as "What a Wonderful World" and "Hello Dolly." ● The ingenuity of his solos, both vocally and instrumentally, combined with his endearing personality, earned him the nickname "Pops" among

younger jazz musicians. Louis Armstrong died on July 6, 1971, and was buried with the solemnity and fanfare of the traditional New Orleans style funeral. He remains one of the most famous of all American jazz musicians. ● Armstrong was a true innovator among the collection of ten jazz musicians in the Legends of American Music series. The Louis Armstrong stamp was illustrated by Dean Mitchell of Overland Park, Kansas.

ARMSTRONG

Background: "Portr
of Louis"

Inset, above: Louie'
early cornet

Opposite, top left:
Early LPs including
the Hot Five, first
European concert
recording

Opposite, right:
Showing the way,
Corona, Queens,
New York, 1968

Opposite, bottom left:
Early record labels

Place
Stamp
Here

It was 1945 — at long last, the year of victory. After four long years fighting a war on two fronts, the boys were coming home. It had been a year of great hardship and loss for the forces on both sides. ● After turning back the last great counteroffensive by the Germans in the Battle of the Bulge, the Allies had Hitler's army in retreat in Europe. In the Pacific, however, the Allied advance was meeting heavy resistance. Few Japanese soldiers or sailors surrendered, preferring death in the name of the Emperor to the shame of surrender. Sustaining heavy casualties on Iwo Jima, the U.S. Marines raised the Stars and Stripes on February 23, and finally defeated the Japanese forces on March 26. General Douglas MacArthur's forces had landed on Luzon, the main island of the Philippines, in January and, after fierce fighting, liberated Manila on March 3. From April through June, thousands of American Marines, GIs and sailors gave their lives to win the last big campaign of the Pacific — the battle for Okinawa. ● In Europe, Soviet troops and American GIs finally linked up at the Elbe River on April 25. A new kind of horror awaited advancing Allied troops in the first months of 1945. The liberation of scores of Nazi camps saw tens of thousands of emaciated Holocaust survivors greet Allied soldiers with sunken eyes, famished bodies and blank stares. For much of the world, this was the first graphic evidence of the systematic roundup and murder of millions of people, about six million of them Jews, in death and concentration camps. ● The German High Command finally surrendered at Reims on May 7. With millions of war-weary refugees uprooted by the fighting or forced to go to Germany as laborers, Europe and the Allies went about the task of reset-

tlement. ● Harry S. Truman had succeeded Franklin D. Roosevelt as President on April 12. In early August, atomic bombs exploded on Hiroshima and Nagasaki. Soon thereafter, on August 14, Truman announced Japan's surrender. The long-awaited news brought celebrations to the streets and towns of the United States. The official surrender was signed on September 2, which was designated V-J Day. The returning fighting men and women were welcomed home as heroes. ● This fifth and final ten-stamp miniature sheet commemorating the 50th anniversary of America's participation in the Allied victory was designed by Bill Bond of Arlington, Virginia.

Opposite, background: V-E Day, New York City, 1945

Top left: Soldiers pull copies of *Stars And Stripes* as they come off the press of *The London Times* at 9 p.m. on May 7, 1945

Right: D-day forces assault Iwo Jima

Bottom: Seventh Army soldiers pose atop the barrel of a German 274 mm railroad gun

WAR II

Place
Stamps
Here

JAZZ

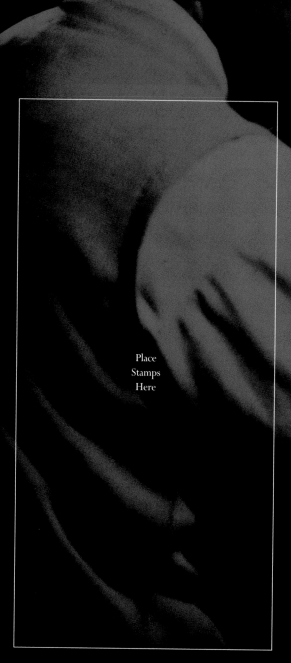

Background: "The Underdog," bassist Charles Mingus

Inset above: Early LPs

Opposite, top left: Ragtime pianist Eubie Blake tinkles the keys, 1980

Opposite, right: Bird lives, alto saxophone bopper Charlie "Yardbird" Parker

Opposite, bottom left: Tenor saxophone giant John Coltrane

Place
Stamps
Here

MUSICIANS

They lived for the music. Each one in pursuit of that one sound, that one style, that was fresh, new and original. And they did it all in the name of that uniquely American music we call "jazz." ● As jazz great Wynton Marsalis once said, "The sharing of ideas that takes place on the bandstand is a musical metaphor for the type of exchange that the best in community living inspires." Those ideas were not only shared but created by these founding fathers of jazz — pianists Eubie Blake, Jelly Roll Morton, James P. Johnson, Erroll Garner and Thelonious Monk; saxophonists Coleman Hawkins, Charlie "Bird" Parker and John Coltrane; and bassist Charles Mingus. ● If there is one common thread that binds the innovative contributions of these musicians, it is their relentless pursuit of improvisational originality. From the dawn of the ragtime era in the early teens through the evolution of dixieland, swing, bebop and modal jazz, the practice of instrumental improvisation dominated the playing styles of these remarkable musicians. First came the bouncing, stomping, ragtime recordings of Eubie Blake and Jelly Roll Morton, followed closely by

the "hot" piano sounds of James P. Johnson. The artful arpeggios of tenor saxophonist Coleman Hawkins and pianist Erroll Garner gave rise to

new melodicism in the 40s. Then came the stunning brilliance and speed of alto saxophonist Charlie Parker, who, along with Dizzy Gillespie, ignited the up-tempo sounds of the bebop era. ● Among the most interesting and unusual instrumentalists and composers in

this legendary group are saxophonist John Coltrane, pianist Thelonious Monk and bassist Charles Mingus. Stretching the tonal boundaries of western music scales and functional harmony, these three jazz greats inspired a "third stream" in the evolution of jazz that lasted well into the 1970s. ● This collection of ten jazz artists, illustrated by Thomas Blackshear of Colorado Springs, Colorado, and Dean Mitchell of Overland Park, Kansas, acknowledges the improvisational excellence and dynamic contributions these musical legends made to America's original music — jazz.

Of all nature's miracles, the fall season has a way of reminding us just how magnificent our world of colors can be. For the gardener, too, it's a time for colors anew — the ritual blooms of fall garden flowers. In celebration of this bountiful season, designer Ned Seidler has given life to these five hardy fall garden flowers. ● Wander around any fall garden from Maine to California, and you're likely to notice the aster. From the Latin *astra* or stars, this vibrant fall flower's name describes the shape of its head. ● The chrysanthemum, recently given the scientific name *Dendranthema,* is perhaps the most popular and most varied of all fall garden flowers. Boasting a wide array of colors, the chrysanthemum doubles extremely well as both a garden flower and a fresh cut bloom. Commonly called "mums," these hardy perennials provide glorious blooms that include those of the Shasta Daisy, Marguerite, Nippon and Painted Daisy. ● One of the most popular stops in any stroll through the fall garden is at the dahlias. Originally native to Central America, the dahlia was named to honor the Swedish botanist Andreas Dahl. Of its twenty-seven species, the dahlia offers such a stunning variety of sizes and colors that it rivals the popularity of even the rose. ● "...I'm over here...in the hydrangea bush!" By the time Donna Reed proclaimed her whereabouts to Jimmy Stewart in the classic American film *It's a Wonderful Life*, many hydrangeas had become a staple of the fall garden. Popular as potted plants as well as great candidates for hardy shrubs, the hydrangea, or hortensia, boasts a variety of blooms throughout North and South America. ● You can't help noticing the rudbeckia. This daisy-like flower includes roughly 25 species and is commonly found in the gardens of the North and Northeast. As fall advances, one rudbeckia remains full of life — boasting the rich, dark center and golden yellow petals that have so fittingly earned it the common name, "Black-eyed Susan."

ASTER

NET WT. 125 mg

MARMALADE
RUDBECKIA

$1.69

Blazing Color

THE

NOVEMBER
1885

AMERICAN
GARDEN

GARDEN

Place
Stamps
Here

Background:
Mammoth asters
from "Childs Seed
Catalog," 1915

Inset, above:
Garden tools

Opposite, right:
Aster and rudbeckia
seed packets

Opposite, bottom:
"The American
Garden," *Journal
of Horticulture,*
November 1885

FLOWERS

REPUBLIC

Far beyond Hawaii's beaches is a jewel of the Pacific whose centuries old coral reefs make it one of the world's most sought after spots for diving. Welcome to the Republic of Palau. ● Teeming with salt water fish of every variety, the reefs surrounding the Palauan islands are a snorkeling and diving paradise. Deep blue, crystal clear waters tease those

who fly over the islands with a taste of what is to come. ● With the Philippines to the west, Indonesia directly to the south and the island of Yap to the northeast, the Republic of Palau is home to a people whose mixed ancestry includes Malay, Melanesian and Polynesian. The two native languages spoken prominently are Palauan, a language related to Indonesian, and Sonsorolese-Tobian. English is universally spoken as well. ● Also known as Belau, Palau is a group of 200 islands in the western Pacific Ocean, with a total land area of 188 square miles spread over 400 miles of ocean, with beaches of pure white sand. Coconut palms sway gently in the light tropical breezes. ● Palau's entire population numbers just 17,000 people. Most Palauans live on the six major islands, Babelthuap, Koror,

Angaur, Peleliu, Kayangel and the Southwest Islands. All the islands except Angaur, Kayangel and the Southwest Islands lie within a lagoon formed by a single barrier reef that stretches over 489 square miles. The largest island, Babelthuap, measures 153 square miles. The smallest Palauan islands are just a

few square feet. Koror is the capital of the Republic. ● During World War II, when General Douglas MacArthur led the Allied forces through the Pacific in his desperate campaign to defeat the Japanese, these tiny islands were the site of some of the war's fiercest fighting. Almost 11,000 men died on the island of Peleliu alone. ● In 1947, after the war ended, Palau became part of the United Nations Trust Territory of the Pacific Islands, under United States administration. The islands remained a Trust Territory for nearly half a century until, on October 1, 1994, the Palau islands gained independence, thus becoming the Republic of Palau. ● In commemoration of the newly established independence of the Republic of Palau, designer Herb Kane of Captain Cook, Hawaii, brings us this honorary stamp filled with deep blue greetings from the Republic of Palau.

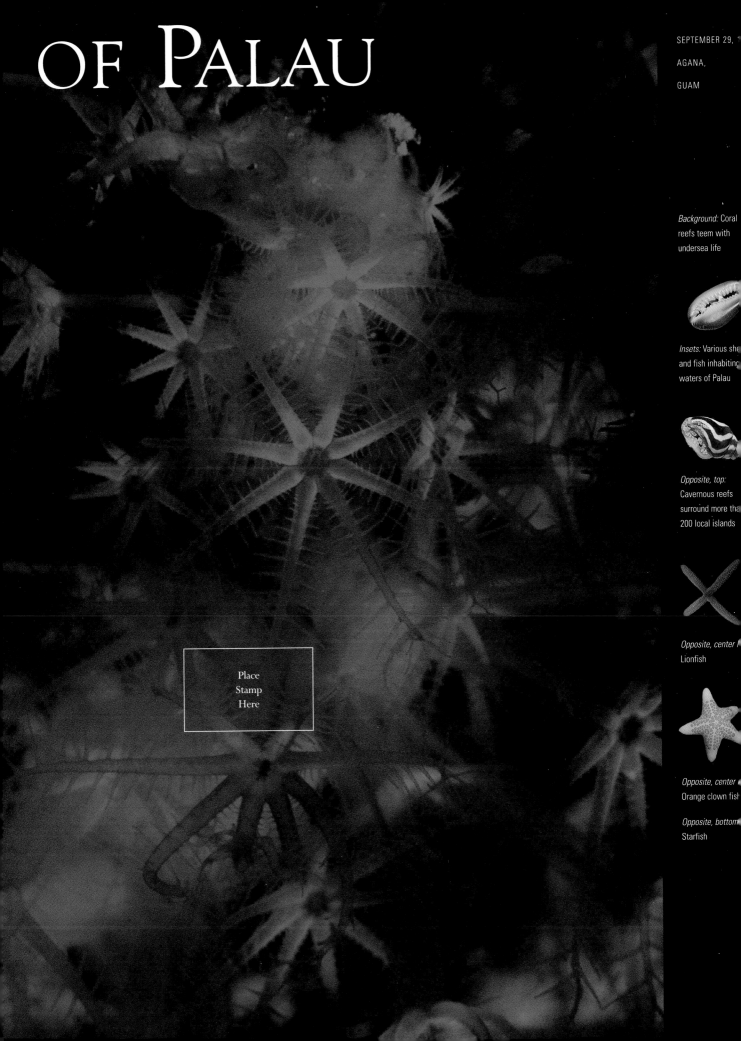

OF PALAU

Background: Coral
reefs teem with
undersea life

Insets: Various she
and fish inhabiting
waters of Palau

Opposite, top:
Cavernous reefs
surround more tha
200 local islands

Opposite, center
Lionfish

Opposite, center
Orange clown fish

Opposite, bottom
Starfish

Place
Stamp
Here

COMIC

Place
Stamps
Here

STRIP CLASSICS

Remember flipping through the funny pages in search of your favorite comic strip? It's been almost a hundred years since Americans started making the comics a favored part of their daily reading diet. Back then, comics were quick glimpses into the life and times of our favorite characters — a crew whose artist/creators brought laughter and levity into our daily lives and our daily newspapers. ● Just for laughs, there were the early favorites like *The Yellow Kid, The Katzenjammer Kids, Barney Google, Bringing Up Father, Krazy Kat* and *Thimble Theatre featuring Popeye*. But it wasn't long before comic relief turned to action and adventure in such classics as *Dick Tracy, Terry and the Pirates, Brenda Starr* and the futuristic *Flash Gordon*. ● By the mid-1950s, comic strips such as these appeared in over 1,500 of the nation's daily newspapers — attracting more than 100 million readers. Gutsy, colorful classics like *Blondie, Alley Oop, Li'l Abner, Gasoline Alley, Toonerville Folks* and *Prince Valiant* exposed the United States' breakfast browsers to glimpses of the hero and heroine, the naive and cynical, as well as both the well educated and the blue-collar worker. All were unique characters whose antics and emotions mirrored the triumphs and challenges that confronted American life during those times. ● Among those comic strip personalities were *Nancy, Little Nemo in Slumberland* and *Little Orphan Annie*. These were characters who freely expressed their inner fears, emotions and expectations. Perhaps the attraction, for so many people, was that somewhere among all these characters was something we saw in ourselves...or someone we aspired to be. ● In a retrospective honoring the one hundredth anniversary of *The Yellow Kid*, 20 different stamps designed by Carl Herrman of Ponte Vedra Beach, Florida, feature these cherished comic favorites.

Background: Toonerville sketch awaits final rendering

Top: Dick Tracy mystery game cards

Center: Skeezix card game characters

Bottom: Barney Google and Spark Plug board game

A MERRY CHRISTMAS
To wish you all the
joys and toys that
Santa Claus can carry!

Christmas past meets Christmas present. This year, it's a celebration of the Victorian and Edwardian eras — a time when almost everything was carefully handcrafted, even the Christmas toys. From puppets and dolls to trucks and trains, the legendary toy makers of the Victorian and Edwardian eras took special pride in making gifts that were intended for one...but would eventually be passed from generation to generation. As busy as the toy makers were, so too were the early publishers of the Christmas card. In their heyday, energetic young publishing companies like Raphael Tuck & Sons and James Campbell & Son created fanciful holiday scenes on greeting cards, writing tablets, puzzles, calendars, paper dolls and postcards — the inspiration for this year's collection of Holiday stamps. ● Four treasured holiday designs from these eras — Santa going down the chimney, fixing a sled, a boy and his tree, and a child with a handmade puppet — bring back the joy of giving and provide a glimpse of the past. These four contemporary issues were adapted and designed by John Grossman and Laura Alders of Richmond Point, California. ● 1995's traditional issue features Giotto's enthroned *Madonna and Child* from the early fourteenth century. Painted during the latter part of Giotto's career, the Madonna and Child were created on wood as the central part of a five-section altarpiece comprising many panels. Against a Byzantine style gold leaf background that symbolizes the realm of heaven, the infant Christ holds his mother's finger innocently as he reaches for her white flower — a traditional symbol of Mary's purity. The Madonna and Child was adapted and designed by veteran stamp designer Richard Sheaff of Boston, Massachusetts.

SEASON

Place
Stamps
Here

Place
Stamp
Here

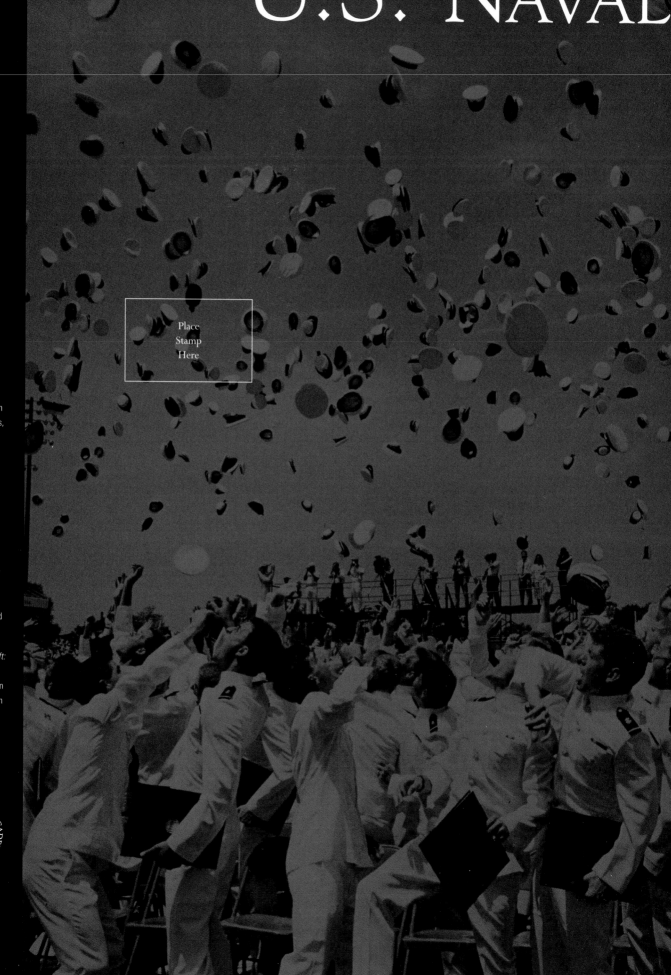

OCTOBER 10, 1995

ANNAPOLIS,
MARYLAND

Place
Stamp
Here

Background:
Officer graduates in
ceremonial hat toss,
Annapolis, MD

Inset, below:
Official Seal, U.S.
Naval Academy

Opposite, top left:
Naval Academy
collar pin

Opposite, top right:
Midshipmen hone
their navigational
charting skills in old
academy study

Opposite, center left:
Naval instructor
teaches midshipmen
the art of navigation

*Opposite, bottom
right:* Leaders of
the brigade of
midshipmen

ACADEMY

This is the training ground for America's best and brightest midshipmen. It is the U.S. Naval Academy, the 150 year old undergraduate college of the U.S. Navy. ● Neatly tucked away in a serene corner of the Chesapeake Bay in the port city of Annapolis, Maryland, the U.S. Naval Academy traces its roots to the mid-1800s when then Secretary of the Navy George Bancroft

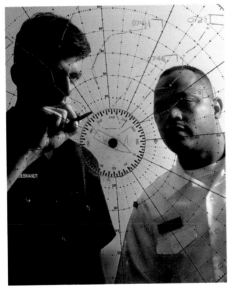

established the first Naval School at Fort Severn in Annapolis in 1845. The Naval School became the United States Naval Academy in 1850. It was there that the earliest American naval tactics and wartime naval maneuvers were developed and taught. ● By the start of World War I, nearly 200 graduates per year became Navy and Marine officers. Today, over 4,000 midshipmen spend four years at Annapolis, training at sea during the summers. On induction day, when each young man and woman takes the oath of office, the undergraduates become plebes. As plebes, they work and study 17 hours a day, learning everything from how to wear a uniform and march in formation to naval aviation, science and engineering; from flag signals and Morse code to calculus, seamanship and navigation. ● The U.S. Naval Academy has grown and changed throughout its 150 years, but its basic mission has remained the same — "To develop midshipmen morally, mentally and physically and to imbue them with the highest ideals of duty, honor and loyalty in order to provide graduates who are dedicated to a career of naval service and have potential for future development in mind and character to assume the highest responsibilities of command, citizenship and government." ● In commemoration of the 150th anniversary of the United States Naval Academy, Dean Ellis of Amagansett, New York, brings us this salute to the midshipmen of the U.S. Navy.

TENNESSEE

Background: On
location, *The Rose
Tattoo*

Inset, above:
Authentic ticket
from New Orleans
streetcar, *Desire*

Opposite, top left:
Hirschfeld drawing

Opposite, right:
Promotional posters
for *A Streetcar
Named Desire, The
Rose Tattoo* and *Cat
on a Hot Tin Roof*

Opposite, bottom left:
Portrait taken during
production of *The
Glass Menagerie*

Place
Stamp
Here

WILLIAMS

"I'm a peculiar blend of the pragmatist, the romanticist and the crocodile," Tennessee Williams said of himself. He was a towering creative force — one of the country's foremost literary figures. • He wrote, Williams said, not for success, but out of "biological necessity." It was from just such necessity that his works bore him two Pulitzer prizes, four New York Drama Critics Circle awards, a Medal of Freedom and numerous other honors. • The characters created by Tennessee Williams embodied emotion — smoldering, twisted and explosive. Stanley Kowalski, Blanche Dubois, Big Daddy, Maggie the Cat — an artistic mix of tenderness with violence, and the cruelty of experience with the kindness of strangers. In his 40 year career, he wrote over 70 plays, 15 movies, two novels, two volumes of poems and countless short stories. • He was born Thomas Lanier Williams on March 26, 1911, in Columbus, Mississippi. His mother, Edwina Estelle Dakin and her children lived with her parents, the Rev. and Mrs. Walter Dakin. Williams' father, Cornelius Coffin Williams, was a loud, aggressive salesman on the road. Finally, he moved the family to St. Louis, in 1918, where Williams recalled his parents fighting bitterly. Many speculate that such domestic fighting inspired Williams' most celebrated works. • After graduating from the University of Iowa in 1938, Williams moved to New Orleans. En route, he stopped to visit his grandparents in Memphis. There, he sought to enter a playwriting contest, but he was too old, so he invented a new identity and birthdate to qualify. Claiming to be from Memphis, he changed his name to Tennessee Williams. • His first play, *Battle of Angels* (1940), was a disaster. It was abandoned after two weeks of tryouts in Boston and never opened in New York. His first major success came with *The Glass Menagerie*, in 1945. It won the New York Drama Critics Circle Award as well as two other awards. Williams later won Pulitzer prizes for *A Streetcar Named Desire* (1948) and *Cat on a Hot Tin Roof* (1955). • In memory of this great American poet and playwright, designer Michael Deas of New Orleans, pays tribute to Tennessee Williams with this stamp — a new addition to the Literary Arts Series.

JAMES

Place
Stamp
Here

Background:
Fremont flag

Inset, below: Polk
banner, 1844

Opposite, top: Portrait
of James Polk by
G.P.A. Healy, 1846

Opposite, right:
"The Young Hickory"
campaign banner

Opposite, middle:
James and Sarah Polk
on the south portico,
1849

K. POLK

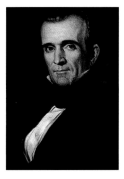

"His capacity for business is great...and to extraordinary powers of labor, both mental and physical, he unites the tact and judgment which are requisite to the successful direction of such an office," wrote former President Andrew Jackson of James K. Polk in 1845. As our 11th President, serving from 1845 to 1849, James Polk was perhaps the most successful President at actually fulfilling his campaign promises. ● Born the son of a Scotch-Irish farmer in 1795 in Mecklenburg County, North Carolina, Polk with his family moved to Tennessee in 1806. After graduating law school with top honors from the University of North Carolina at Chapel Hill, Polk entered politics by serving in the Tennessee legislature. It was there that he was befriended by former President Andrew Jackson. Polk eventually rose to become Speaker of the House of Representatives from 1835 to 1839.

Soon after, Polk left Congress to become Governor of Tennessee, where he publicly declared himself an expansionist by asserting that Texas should be "reannexed" and all of Oregon "reoccupied." ● When the Democratic convention opened in 1845, the leading candidate, former President Martin Van Buren, attempted to avoid the subject of expansionism by declaring himself opposed to the annexation of Texas. With Van Buren and other prominent candidates deadlocked, Polk emerged and was nominated on the ninth ballot. ● "Who is James K. Polk?" the opposition Whig party members shouted in a veiled attempt to paint Polk as a "dark horse" candidate. Their attempts failed when James Polk defeated famed Henry Clay with his strong expansionist platform. ● "There are four great measures which are to be the measures of my administration,"

President Polk said shortly after his Inauguration, "one, a reduction of the tariff; another, the independent treasury; a third, the settlement of the Oregon boundary question; and lastly, the acquisition of California." ● By the end of his administration, he had accomplished all four goals. His first two, the Walker Tariff Act and the Independent Treasury Act, passed Congress and became law in 1846. The Stars and Stripes soon flew in lands from as far westward as Texas, New Mexico and California to as far north as the Puget Sound after Polk's deft negotiations with Mexico and Great Britain. As a result, during Polk's administration, America's size increased by two-thirds. ● With his physical condition failing from hard work, James K. Polk left the Presidency and died in June of 1849. ● This distinguished, engraved presidential stamp was designed in honor of the "dark horse" President by John Thompson of Waterloo, Iowa.

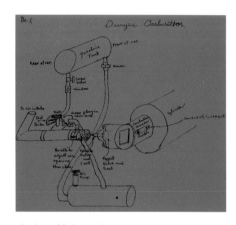

Those marvelous men and their fabulous machines! From buggies, boxcars and bicycles they came, fledgling young inventors whose pursuit was the motorcar. ● Just before the turn of the century, the newfangled machines began to appear, competing for space on streets and country lanes with the more familiar horse and buggy. The motorcars included the 1893 Duryea, 1894 Haynes, 1898 Columbia, 1899 Winton and 1901 White. They emerged from the stables of the carriage and wagon maker, the shops of the bicycle mechanic, the garage of the machine operator and the home of your average "tinkerer." ● The three major features of these five early motorcars had been evolving for decades — tiller steering, the drive train and body styling. Two of the cars, the 1893 Duryea and 1894 Haynes, were prototypes, but, because of their impracticality, they never reached production. The remaining three, the Columbia, Winton and White, are fine examples of motorcars from the earliest production years of the American automobile. All three were adapted from the principles of the motorcar's predecessor, the bicycle. From bicycle technology, their inventors expanded on the narrow wheels and lightweight construction. From the art of carriage coachwork, they took their body designs, whose underlying frames shielded the mechanical features of the motorcar. ● All five motorcars represent the three primary methods of propulsion that were available to United States automobile builders at the time. The Duryea, Haynes and Winton were gasoline powered, the Columbia was electric and the White was steam propelled. Despite their differences, the five serve as excellent examples of the nation's pioneering success in mechanical ingenuity. Their individual advances proved pivotal in establishing the country's dominance in the volume production of automobiles in the years and decades that followed. ● Designer Ken Dallison of Mississauga, Ontario, Canada has re-created these five turn-of-the-century automobiles in a tribute to the spirit of invention they inspire.

NOT FOR SPEEDING . . . *This bicycle cop stopped Elwood Haynes (right hand on that outside brake lever) in 1895 and ordered his horseless carriage off the Chicago streets. Can you hear Haynes' passenger saying, "Well now, Mr. Officer, can't we get together on this thing?"*

AUTOMOBILES

Background: All aboard. Six men in front of the Winton Motor Carriage Co.

Inset, above: Schematic of an early automobile

Opposite, top: White steam carriages, 1901

Opposite, top left: 1899 Winton advertisement. "Traveling is a Pleasure"

Opposite, bottom: Elwood Haynes, inventor, pulled over by bicycle cop, 1895

Opposite, top right: Sketch of groundbreaking Duryea fuel system, 1893

Place
Stamps
Here

Title Page: Herman Leonard

Page 2: Charlotte Dinger Collection

Lunar New Year: 8 (top) ©1995 Max Reid/PhotoAssist, Inc.; (left) from *Domesticated Deities and Auspicious Emblems: The Iconography of Everyday Life in Village China,* by Po Sung-nien and David Johnson, Chinese Popular Culture Project, 1992/Institute of East Asian Studies Publications, University of California, Berkeley, CA, (right) © George Hall/Woodfin Camp & Associates, Inc. 9 (background) ©1995 Max Reid/PhotoAssist, Inc.; (panel) ©1995 Max Reid/PhotoAssist, Inc.

Florida Statehood: 10 (top) Warshaw Collection of Business Americana, Archives

Center, National Museum of American History, Smithsonian Institution; (center left) Larry Downing/Woodfin Camp & Associates, Inc.; (bottom) Library of Congress. 11 (background) © Karen Holzberg; (panel) The Herrman Collection.

Earth Day: 12 (background) Terry Pagos/Folio, Inc.; (panel) Illustrations by Gretchen East. 13 (top) © Grant Black/First Light; (left center, top to bottom) Jessica Feichtl, Stephanie Mason, Joshua Marshall, Eun Sung Yeo/U.S. Postal Service; (right, top to bottom) Katy Maker, Matthew Balestrieri/ U.S. Postal Service; (bottom left) © Grant Black/First Light.

Richard Nixon: 14 (top left) Signature, Courtesy National Archives; (middle left) © Wally

McNamee/Folio, Inc.; (right) ©1972 Time Inc., reprinted with permission; (bottom) Fred Maroon/Folio, Inc. 15 (background) National Archives; (panel) Museum of American Political Life, University of Hartford, photography by Steven Laschever.

Bessie Coleman: 16 (background) © George Hall/Woodfin Camp & Associates, Inc.; Drawings from *Encyclopedia of U.S. Military Aircraft: The World War I Production Program,* by Robert B. Casari, Military Aircraft Publications, ©1975; (panel) From *Practical Aviation* by Charles B. Hayward, American Technical Society, Chicago, 1919/Courtesy of Ken Hyde. 17 (top left) Renée Comet Photography; (top right) Courtesy of Ken Hyde; (middle)

The Bettmann Archive; (bottom left) Courtesy Eartha White Collection, Thomas G. Carpenter Library, University of North Florida, Jacksonville.

Love: 18 (background) *Psyche Brought Back to Life by the Kiss of Amor* by Antonio Canova/Photograph by Erich Lessing from Art Resource; (panel) *The Kiss* by Constantin Brancusi/Giraudon/Art Resource. 19 (top left) *Les Amoreux aux Marguerites* by Marc Chagall/Art Resource; (right) *The Kiss* by Gustav Klimt/Photograph by Erich Lessing from Art Resource; (bottom) *La Cathédrale* by Auguste Rodin/Photograph by Gian Berto Vanni/Art Resource.

Recreational Sports: 20 (top right) Lithograph by Charles Hart from original by Edward

Penfield/Library of Congress; (left) Watercolor by Edward Penfield/Library of Congress; (bottom right) From *Right Down Your Alley,* by Ford Banes, 1946, A.S. Barnes and Co. 21 (background) Archive Photos; (panel) Renée Comet Photography.

POW & MIA: 22 (top) Gordon Clark/Sygma; (center left) Renée Comet Photography; (bottom) © Lloyd Wolf/Folio, Inc. 23 (background) National Archives; (panel) Courtesy of the U.S. Navy Museum, ©1995 Max Reid/PhotoAssist, Inc.

Marilyn Monroe: 24 (top) UPI/ Bettmann; (center left top) Archive Photos/Frank Driggs Collection; (center left bottom) Archive Photos/Frank Driggs Collection; (bottom) Courtesy

PHOTO CREDITS

of The Kobal Collection. 25 (background) Michael Ochs Archives/Venice, CA; (panel) Signature, Courtesy of the Estate of Marilyn Monroe.

Texas Statehood: 26 (background) Library of Congress; (panel) Texas Ranger Museum and Hall of Fame, Waco, TX. 27 (top) Arizona Historical Society, Southern Arizona Division; (center right) Library of Congress; (center left) Whit Bronaugh; (bottom right) Arizona Historical Society, Southern Arizona Division.

Great Lakes Lighthouses: 28 (background) Photograph by Lee Radzak; (overlay) U.S. Army Corps of Engineers; (panel) National Archives. 29 (top) Minnesota Historical Society/Split Rock Lighthouse;

(left) National Archives; (right) U.S. Postal Service.

United Nations: 30 (background) J.P. Laffont/Sygma; (panel) Renée Comet Photography. 31 (top left) Renée Comet Photography; (top right) Ezra Stoller © Esto; (center left) United Nations Photo, John Isaac; (bottom) United Nations Photo, John Isaac.

Civil War: 32 (all) Collection of Don Troiani/Historical Art Prints; © Bob Tracy. 33 (background) Collection of Don Troiani/Historical Art Prints; ©1995 Max Reid/ PhotoAssist, Inc.

Carousel Horses: 34 (background) William Manns Collection; (panel) Scott Landis. 35 (top left) Scott Landis; (top right) Herschell Carousel

Factory Museum; (bottom left) Underwood Collection/ Bettmann Archive; (bottom right) From *Art of the Carousel*, Charlotte Dinger Collection.

Women's Suffrage: 36 (background) FPG International; (panel) Both courtesy of the Smithsonian Institution. 37 (top left) New York Public Library, U.S. History and Genealogy Division, City Views Collection; (right) Library of Congress; (bottom) The Schlesinger Library, Radcliffe College.

Louis Armstrong: 38 (top left) Courtesy of Larry Eanet/© 1995 Max Reid/PhotoAssist, Inc.; (right) Courtesy of the Louis Armstrong House and Archives at Queens College, CUNY; (bottom left) Library of Congress/©1995 Max Reid/ PhotoAssist, Inc. 39 (back-

ground) Archive Photos/London Daily Express; (panel) Richard Hunt Photography.

World War II: 40 (top left) Imperial War Museum, London; (right) National Archives; (bottom) National Archives. 41 (background) UPI/Bettmann.

Jazz Musicians: 42 (background) Lee Tanner Photography; (panel) Courtesy of Larry Eanet/©1995 Max Reid/PhotoAssist, Inc. 43 (top left) Archive Photos/Tim Boxer; (right) Herman Leonard; (bottom left) © Chuck Stewart.

Garden Flowers: 44 Renée Comet Photography; *The American Garden,* from the Warshaw Collection of Business Americana, Archives Center, National Museum of

American History, Smithsonian Institution; (right) ©1995 Max Reid/PhotoAssist, Inc. 45 (background) From *Childs Seed Catalog,* 1915 From the Warshaw Collection of Business Americana, Archives Center, National Museum of American History, Smithsonian Institution; (panel) Renée Comet Photography.

Republic of Palau: 46 (top) © David Hiser/Photographers Aspen; (left) © William W. Hartley; (right) © Ed Robinson/Pacific Stock; (bottom, left) © Ed Robinson/ Pacific Stock; (bottom, right) © Dave B. Fleetham/Pacific Stock. 47 (background) © William W. Hartley; (panel, shells) Renée Comet Photography; (panel, starfish top) © Ed Robinson/Pacific

Stock, (panel, starfish bottom) © Dave B. Fleetham/Pacific Stock.

Comic Strip Classics: 48 and 49 (all) From Collection of Rick Marschall/Renée Comet Photography.

Holiday Season: 50 (middle left) From the Hallmark Archives and Design Collections, Hallmark Cards, Inc.; (top, middle and bottom) Courtesy of the Washington Doll's House and Toy Museum, Washington, D.C./Renée Comet Photography. 51 (background) Stan Barouh; (panel) Courtesy of the Washington Doll's House and Toy Museum, Washington, D.C./Renée Comet Photography.

U.S. Naval Academy: 52 (background) Courtesy U.S. Naval Academy, Photography

Branch; (panel) U.S. Naval Academy. 55 (top left) U.S. Naval Academy/©1995 Max Reid/PhotoAssist, Inc.; (top right) U.S. Naval Academy, Special Collections; (center left) Courtesy U.S. Naval Academy, Photography Branch; (bottom right) Courtesy U.S. Naval Academy, Photography Branch.

Tennessee Williams: 54 (background) © Academy of Motion Picture Arts and Sciences, photograph by Sanford Roth/from the Sanford Roth Collection; (panel) Collection of Richard Freeman Leavitt/© 1995 Max Reid/ PhotoAssist, Inc. 55 (top left) © Al Hirschfeld. Drawing reproduced by special arrangement with Hirschfeld's exclusive representative, The Margo Feiden Galleries, Ltd., New

York; (right, top to bottom) Photofest; Photofest/Jagarts; Photofest/Jagarts; Photofest; (bottom left) Photography Collection, Harry Ransom Humanities Research Center, The University of Texas at Austin.

James K. Polk: 56 (background) Courtesy of the Southwest Museum, Los Angeles, Photo #CT-10; (panel) Courtesy of the Smithsonian Institution. 57 (top left) Portrait painted by George Peter Alexander Healy, circa 1846/Courtesy of the James K. Polk Memorial Association, Columbia, TN; (right) Courtesy of George Eastman House; (bottom) Courtesy of the James K. Polk Memorial Association, Columbia, TN.

Antique Automobiles: 58

(left, all) Western Reserve Historical Society; (top right) Smithsonian Institution. 59 (background) Reprinted with permission of the American Automobile Manufacturers Association; (panel) Western Reserve Historical Society.

Page 64: UPI/Bettmann.

Envelope Front: Marilyn Monroe: Michael Ochs Archive/Venice, CA. Hat toss: U.S. Naval Academy. Louis Armstrong: Archive Photos/ London Daily Express.

Envelope Back: Carousel: Charlotte Dinger Collection. V-E Day: UPI/Bettmann.

These stamps and this stamp collecting book were produced by Stamp Services, United States Postal Service, Marvin Runyon, Postmaster General

and Chief Executive Officer; Loren E. Smith, Chief Marketing Officer and Senior Vice President; Azeezaly S. Jaffer, Manager, Stamp Services.

Special thanks to the Stamp Services team and for key contributions by: Terry McCaffrey for project management; Paul Ovchinnikoff for print supervision; Wanda Parks for contract administration.

Consultants: Photo Assist for visual and historical research and authentication. Contractors: Grafik Communications, Ltd. for artistic direction, design and layout; Alan Schulman for writing.